Sadomasochism
in Art and Politics

Dr Estela V. Welldon

CONTENTS

ACKNOWLEDGMENTS

I am grateful to David Scrase for his kind editorial assistance. I owe many thanks to Brett Kahr, whose invaluable help has been essential for the completion of this book.
Finally, this book would not have been possible without the editorial and self-publishing talents of Alex Goforth.

Cover painting by Ricardo Cinalli

1 'THE LOVING WEEKEND ON ST VALENTINE'S DAY'

As a practising psychiatrist who has specialised in dealing with criminality and perversion, I have never ceased to be surprised by the great variety of ways in which people express their psychological distress. All the patients that I have seen have come to my office and have talked to me about their extreme or bizarre sexual behaviours, but I had never actually witnessed them acting out such activities in my presence.

When I started writing this book, I suddenly remembered one particular occasion a few years ago when I saw unusual sexual practices performed before my very eyes. I had been invited by a television network to participate in a late-night programme called 'The Loving Weekend on St Valentine's Day'. I was asked in my professional capacity as a psychiatrist to explain to the viewers the dynamics operating in sadomasochistic activities. The TV researchers had interviewed quite a number of individuals involved in all sorts of sadomasochistic relationships as possible guests to appear on television. Unsurprisingly, the researchers had more people volunteering to do this than they had anticipated. This left them in the enviable position of choosing whoever or whatever they considered to be the most bizarre or complicated sexual scenario. As they explained to me over the phone, one of the chosen scenarios involved three characters, all of whom were young, attractive, articulate people, who claimed to have achieved a perfect balance in their daily lives through a certain spicy routine. This threesome consisted of a placid, acquiescent husband, a dominatrix wife and a young, single man, who had eagerly taken on the role of the 'slave', 'victim' and ultimately 'dog'. Their routine consisted of a fixed pattern in which the wife would dominate the amorous young fellow who responded exclusively to any of 'Madam's' requirements and whims involving verbal and physical abuse, all of which provided the three-some with much pleasure. The young man's only requirement was to be the Madam's slave. The husband said this arrangement was ideally suited to his own needs because, in this way, he felt freed from a demanding, possessive and jealous wife.

During the live interview they explained to the

captivated audience the intricacies of their relationship. The three of them were very indignant about any idea or 'false' understanding that this behaviour might be linked to early traumatic experiences or that any of the threesome had been the recipients of some suffering in their early lives. On the contrary, they claimed vigorously that this series of activities was meant to enlighten and to enhance love and sex among themselves. The use of different clothes and role-playing was yet another device to add more excitement and liveliness.

They spoke with a strong sense of confidence and determination, especially concerning the essential ingredient – that is, the consensual characteristic present in all their interactions. This, according to them, blatantly demonstrated that there was no humiliation or pain inflicted; on the contrary, it had to do with purity, love and truth. They were opposed to the term 'sadomasochism' and, rather, used the term 'sub-dominance', since in their view the sadist does not enjoy hurting people but what he or she enjoys is giving pleasure to the other. In this case, the 'slave' was the shared 'enjoyment piece' for the dominatrix woman and her husband. Despite this obvious dehumanisation, or perhaps because of it, the young fellow gleefully added that he was delighted with this arrangement. While the interview was taking place on camera, they began to act out their roles, with the 'slave' being blindfolded by the 'dominatrix', who also placed a collar around his neck, making him look like a little dog. He was crawling around her, and while being whipped he began to massage her in an adoring way. He said he did enjoy humiliation, adding, 'I accept how submissive I am', and later, 'Madam is the most important person for me in the world. This is nothing to do with sex anyway.'

In addition to this unusual threesome performing live on television, there was a fourth party present, another practising sadomasochist. This woman was an attractive young lesbian involved in prostitution, specialising in the field as a dominatrix of men. She told us how she concentrated on giving pleasure to her clients or 'punters' by inflicting pain on them through performing different learnt techniques. She showed a great deal of ability and experience when talking at length of the need in her 'chosen' profession to be in the controlling situation, which she qualified as producing 'a sense of purity'. She added that it was dangerous only when two people had not properly learnt what they were about to do. She even compared this sense of 'complicity' to the

4

successful separation between mother and baby, which can be accomplished only when both parties, mother and child, are able to trust one another, 'to be loved and to be cosseted by each other'. She added, 'You not only have to be in control but also have to inspire a sense of trust and then they do not take any risks.'

This woman felt a great sense of empowerment while at her work which would immediately result in increasing her self-esteem, though this was short-lived. It is not coincidental that she herself had been a victim of paternal incest. As we can observe, her 'chosen' way of resolving this early sexual abuse was, first, not to trust men – by implicitly withdrawing altogether from intimate heterosexual relationships. Second, she would make her living out of administering physical punishment and humiliation to men who requested or were in need of this kind of 'treatment'. In this way, she was not only taking symbolic revenge against her father's abuse but also protecting herself from any emotional closeness to men. At the same time, she was giving them pleasure and pleasing them – a 'compromise formation' as Freud calls it, in which two opposite intentions or tendencies are expressed in the same activity. A fixed and rigid contractual agreement would give the two parties involved a 'necessary' guarantee of safety. She was, of the four of them, certainly the most accessible to any real understanding of whatever was going on in her internal world. She could actually acknowledge the existence of her own internal world, and this would allow her to venture to look at her past, making some connections with her early history. Meanwhile, the other three were unable to make any such connection. One could assume, but of course, without any firm evidence, that their strong denial was the only tolerable defence mechanism available to them because of very early and severe disturbances.

This new experience, of seeing sadomasochist practices in front of my eyes for the first time, helped me to appreciate the seemingly consensual nature of these practices. I was surprised at how contained these four individuals seemed to be, and, unlike the patients in my clinical practice who asked for my help, none of these television guests had ever felt the need for professional help.

Sadomasochism is a complicated concept, so much so that in the 'Bible' of psychiatric classifications, the *Diagnostic and Statistical Manual of Mental Disorders* of the American Psychiatric

Association (1994), the term is not even listed in the index. Instead, psychiatrists divide the term into its two component parts – sexual sadism and sexual masochism. Gilles Deleuze strongly claims that sadism and masochism do not together constitute a single entity: 'They are not respectively made up of partial impulses, but each is complete in itself.'[1]

Interestingly enough, at the beginning of the century, before sadism was adopted as an official psychiatric term, the noted psychopathologist Albert von Schrenck-Notzing introduced the term *algolagnia*, which meant the lust for pain, and although it defined the desire to cause pain as an end in itself, it did not make any differentiation between sadism and masochism.

2 SEXUAL SADISM

Everybody everywhere trying to express hurt, humiliation and pain inflicted or suffered in relationships liberally uses the words sadism and masochism. But what is the real meaning attached to them? The term 'sadism' is associated with activities, usually of a sexual nature, involving the infliction of pain on another person, providing sexual satisfaction to the person who inflicts the pain. According to *DSM-IV*, the official manual of psychiatric classifications:

Sadistic fantasies or acts may involve activities that indicate the dominance of the person over the victim (e.g. forcing the victim to crawl or keeping the victim in a cage). They may also involve restraint, blindfolding, paddling, spanking, whipping, pinching, beating, burning, electrical shocks, rape, cutting, stabbing, strangulation, torture, mutilation or killing. Sadistic sexual fantasies are likely to have been present in childhood.

Traditionally these actions always include other persons, who could be consensual partners or unsuspecting victims.

When considering sexual sadism, it is important to notice the difference made between sadistic *fantasies* and sadistic *actions*. Perversions are defined predominantly as actions, rather than fantasies. In other words, anyone is 'allowed' to indulge in sexual fantasies of any kind without the 'danger' of being categorised as a pervert. Richard von Krafft-Ebing, the eminent Austrian sexologist, first used the term 'sadism', which he derived from the surname of the 18th-century author the Marquis de Sade, a man who devoted his writings to depictions of brutal and cruel sexual actions, recording them in the most beautiful and lyrical manner. He himself had been involved in many of these activities, which was part of the reason for his being sent to prison. In prison, he continued to use them as fantasies to stimulate his fertile imagination in his extremely disturbing, but also influential, work. De Sade's writing became a source of inspiration to innovative and even revolutionary artwork. I am reminded here of a felicitous comment from Dr Joyce McDougall, the doyenne of French psychoanalysts, that 'humankind's leading "erotogenic zone" is located in the mind', and she courageously adds that 'perversion, like beauty, is in the eye of the beholder'. [2]

3 MARQUIS DE SADE

The Marquis de Sade, who lived throughout the French Revolution, spent a third of his life in prison, where he did most of his writing. Born in 1740, he has become the mentor of many artists, writers and film makers of the modern age: André Masson's fetishistic paintings of male and female sex organs; George Bataille's erotic fantasies; Luis Buñuel's *Belle de Jour*, in which Severine, the heroine played by Catherine Deneuve, expresses her masochism in daydreams of Sadeian humiliation and torture; David Lynch's *Blue Velvet* (1986), with its Sadeian overtones concentrating on the compulsive milieu of perverse desire.3 Other writers such as Baudelaire, Dali, Genet and Foucault are just a few who have commemorated with their own artistic achievements de Sade's original ideas.

De Sade was born a nobleman and died very poor in 1814 in a lunatic asylum. This somewhat paradoxical position is maintained throughout his life. Most of his creativity and freedom of ideas took place while he was in prison. There he was able to write about freedom while experiencing claustrophobia. Prison may have deterred him from acting out his extreme sexual fantasies, but it did not succeed in deterring him from expressing his thoughts and fantasies in most elegant ways in his writings, which push the boundaries of taste to extreme limits. Incidentally, there is a strong possibility that the 'safety' of his imprisonment facilitated this ability. He was aptly regarded as the ultimate rebel. De Sade had a very unhappy childhood, being the witness of much domestic violence. At the age of five, his family life was utterly disrupted when his mother decided to leave home. Since his father was often absent, spending long periods abroad in his position as diplomat, he was sent to live with his uncle, who was a priest. Very soon, he became aware of the hypocrisy of the church and began to find blasphemy appealing. Actual blasphemy and transgressive sexuality, either in fantasy or in action, were to be continued all through his life and became from then on his favourite occupations, to an obsessional degree. At the age of 14, he was sent to boarding school, where he was subjected to much physical punishment. His marriage was an arranged one, and it was short-lived because of his subversive activities, which included various and numerous incidents of sexual abuse and assaults on his wife, which his mother-in-law deeply resented. Eventually she managed through her active intervention to have him sent to prison.

De Sade's writings – in particular, *Justine* (1791), *Philosophy in the Bedroom* (1795), *The 120 Days of Sodom* (1785) and *Juliette* (1798) – are extraordinary, daring attempts to push bourgeois morality to extremes and to undress it from all its hypocrisy. At first glance, *Justine* and *Juliette* appear to be at opposite poles of the psychological spectrum, yet a closer look reveals that at the same time they reflect and complement one another – just as the two polarities of sadism and masochism become unconsciously the same. They were written just before the French revolution: Justine poses as a female masochist being constantly humiliated. Her bitter reward is to exemplify that the victim is always morally superior to the master. Juliette, on the other hand, exploits her sexuality to the extreme; she is the exception, and she is a superwoman in the Nietzschian sense, transcending her gender but not its contradictions. She is a terrorist of love and motherhood, using, abusing, exploiting and neglecting lovers and child as she wishes, according to her own whimsical moods.

The 120 Days of Sodom is set in the 17th century, and in it de Sade describes in intimate detail the most horrific things people can do to one another during a murderous holiday financially sponsored by profits made from the Thirty Years War. The book inspired Pier Paolo Passolini for his film *Salo*, which clearly portrays the horrors and cruelty inflicted to non-consensual victims. Its viewing, regardless of its artistic qualities, becomes a sadistic attack on the viewer, who has been unwittingly transformed into a consensual victim.

4 DE SADE'S 'CONTRIBUTION' TO FEMINISM

It is fascinating to observe how contemporary women writers, among them many ardent feminists, react in totally opposing ways to de Sade's ideas. Some strongly repudiate his view of women, considering him a monster and a lecherous pornographer; others, perhaps surprisingly, celebrate his work on the grounds that it concerns the nature of freedom of sexuality for both genders. According to the latter, he refuses to consider women as just reproductive machines and apportions them the freedom to be sexual beings. Camille Paglia, the American academic feminist, believes de Sade to be a major intellectual and considers his book *Justine* one of the great masterpieces. On the other hand, Janine Chasseguet-Smirgel, one of the most prominent French psychoanalysts working in the field of perversions, says that women in de Sade's work are made objects of the greatest contempt; the female sex is not only viewed as an object of repulsion but also compared in denigrating terms to the anus, which, called the 'other temple', is greatly idealised by de Sade for its function as the expeller of end products (that is, faeces).

Man Ray, one of the best representatives of surrealism, shows in a 1933 photograph his abhorrence of Catholicism and his contempt for sex as the monopoly on procreative acts by inverting a crucifix and superimposing it on the cleft of a man's buttocks. This is a tribute to de Sade's ideology, which he called 'Monument to D.A.F. Sade', where he demonstrates de Sade's disapproval of reproductive sex and his preference for the practice of sodomy.[4] It is, of course, essential to remember that sodomy was criminalised in France at the time de Sade wrote.

Janine Chasseguet-Smirgel, has used the 'Sadeian setting' to conceptualise her own view of perversion as a universe where utter confusion reigns, whose main feature is the fundamental desire to obliterate the difference between the sexes. Every- body is the same; there are neither males nor females, neither children nor adults. (She reminds us at the beginning of her paper of de Sade's statement: 'And it is to increase my homage that I make distinction neither between ages nor sexes.'[5]) Incest is no longer taboo, and anality is given supremacy as the most potent of libidinal encounters. Women's femininity is annihilated; there is no room for female genitality. She carefully takes us to *The 120 Days of Sodom* – written in 1785 with its emphasis on claustrophobic, circular places and constructions, narrow passages with sphincters – to conclude that 'the pleasure connected to transgression is sustained by the fantasy of having reduced the object to excrement, in breaking down barriers which separate mother from son, daughter from father, brother from sister, the erotogenous zones from each other'[6] and so on, in an attempt to create a new world displacing natural laws. Reality no longer exists, and an illusionary world has been created, placing priority on the importance of both suspense and of codes of laws or regulations.

I had the good fortune of meeting Angela Carter through my close friend Marina Warner following the publication of my book Mother Madonna Whore in 1998. I immediately recognised that Angela, like Marina, possessed extraordinary - Rolls-Royce like - intelligence, and much creativity, originality and passion. Both were close colleagues who had a mutual, deeply respectful friendship, and held each other in high esteem and with great affection. In Angela I also identified the same fearlessness with which I endeavour to approach the world. Angela Carter challenges all other feminists to look at de Sade's writings with a new approach. In her book *The Sadeian Woman* (1979), she puts forward the hypothesis that he treats all sexuality as a political reality and that this is the reason for his being sent to social confinement. Through his work, she writes, he exposes a society and a system of extreme social relations that was in operation in the 'ancient regime' of France. The libertines of that time were great aristocrats, some were landowners, and others were attached to the church or to banking. In other words, his libertines regulated and maintained a society external to themselves where their own institutions had been corrupted and become the embodiment of perversions. According to Carter, de Sade considers the facts of female sexuality not as a moral dilemma but as a political reality. De Sade's heroines, the female libertines, have no inner life, no introspection, and their only role models are libertine men who accept damnation – meaning by this, exile from the world as a necessity of life. In a most provocative way, Carter asserts:

... de Sade declares himself unequivocally for the right of women to fuck ... He urges women to fuck as actively as they are able, so that powered by their enormous and hitherto untapped sexual energy they will then be able to fuck their way into history and, in so doing, change it.[7]

I wonder at the great delight Carter would have in learning that two young women, who seem to be the most fitting match for de Sade, are responsible for writing and producing 'the most graphic film about sex and violence ever made for a general audience',[8] *Baise-Moi* (2000). The French novelist Virginie Despentes wrote the book with the same title, and porn actress Coralie Trinh Thi is her collaborator in a courageous, startling, low-budget movie that has already created a media outcry everywhere it has been shown. This response, they claim, was completely unexpected by them. And the mixed reception didn't stop there. The film was withdrawn when it was first shown in France with a 16 rating, such was the hatred that it provoked in a lot of people, including feminists; however, others supported it to the extent that the minister of culture decided to change the law. It took a year before the film re-opened with a new 18 certificate. The British Board of Film Classification has been ahead of the times, and of French standards of liberalism in sexuality, by giving it an 18 certificate, after cutting one 'unacceptable show' in the film's violent rape scene for its 'extreme sexual imagery'. The piece was acknowledged as a serious and well-made film.

In an interview with the *Financial Times* film critic Nigel Andrews, the makers candidly talk about the film, which portrays two women who embark on a cross-country killing spree as a direct result of one of them being raped and the other being made witness to the shooting of her best friend. It concerns their reaction to humiliation and violence, usually perpetrated by the male gender. When asked if the film is a 'reverse rape' in which men become the targets of the women's need for bitter revenge, their answer corresponds exactly to de Sade's sentiments. They stress that they kill every symbol of oppression – oppression by the police, by the intellectual bourgeoisie and even oppression by stupidity and boredom. After all, when the two women meet, they know they will die, so 'the film is extreme but romantic. *It is about what happens when life fails you and you cross the line.*' This last line is emphasised to indicate once more the degree of synchronicity, or shall I say serendipity, that this contemporary female statement has with the Marquis de Sade and all other followers of the same school. 'Then there's the question of the actresses,' Despentes asserts. 'Of course it's fine to have porn films and porn actresses, but when you put them in a naturalistic drama that causes all kinds of problems. Why? Because you've destroyed the idea that they are sexual toys and brought them to life.

'Me and Coralie,' explains Despentes, 'we didn't go to any of the grandes écoles [the French equivalent of Oxbridge], we didn't do classic cinema studies, we both have strong links with the so-called margins of society, so everything about us was deeply disturbing to the cinematic and media industries. If we'd had the conventional French attitude – you know, conceptual discourse, the right references, something a little less visceral and more intellectual – they would have been reassured. Instead, we were simply too raw, too real for them. Of course, they want to make films about people like us, but they don't want us in their cosy little cinematic world.

'The real problem,' she continues, 'is that *Baise-*

Moi is a film about violent "lower class" women, made by supposedly marginal women. The mainstream doesn't want to hear about people with nothing, the disenfranchised, the marginals, taking up arms and killing people for fun and money. It happens, of course, but we're not allowed to acknowledge it.'

It is interesting to notice that the writings of not only de Sade but also all his followers depict sexual transgressions corresponding to social and political oppression. For example, de Sade had no qualms in referring to anal sex in rewarding and idealised ways, while at that time sodomy was criminalised in France.

In her most compelling and disturbing book, *The Piano Teacher* (made into a prize-winning film), to which I shall refer later, the Austrian writer Elfriede Jelinek achieves her aim of clearly demon- strating that Austria is a closet of Nazi histories with a host of sexual perversions. As I wrote in my 1988 book, *Mother, Madonna, Whore*:

The aetiology of perversion ... is intertwined with the politics of power; one aspect is psychobiological and the other social. It is possible that this difference of response about mothers' abusive actions against their offspring is caused by society's inability to see [a] woman as a complete human being. The difficulties in acknowledging that mothers can abuse their power could be the result of total denial, as a way of dealing with this unpalatable truth.[9]

5 SEXUAL MASOCHISM

The 19th-century Austrian sexologist Richard von Krafft-Ebing not only coined the term 'sadism' but also that of its opposite, 'masochism'. According to Krafft-Ebing:

Masochism is the opposite of sadism. While the latter is the desire to cause pain and use force, the former is the wish to suffer pain and be subjected to force.

I feel justified in calling this sexual anomaly 'masochism' because the author Sacher-Masoch frequently made this perversion, which up to his time was quite unknown to the scientific world as such, the substratum of his writings.

According to *DSM-IV*:

The paraphiliac focus of Sexual Masochism involves the act (real, not simulated) of being humiliated, beaten, bound or otherwise made to suffer. Some individuals are bothered by their masochistic fantasies, which may be invoked during sexual inter- course or masturbation but not otherwise acted on. In such cases, the masochistic fantasies usually involve being raped while being held or bound by others so that there is no possibility of escape. Others act on the masochistic sexual urges by themselves (e.g. binding themselves, sticking them- selves with pins, shocking themselves electrically or self-mutilation) or with a partner. Masochistic acts that may be sought with a partner include restraint (physical bondage), blindfolding (sensory bondage), paddling, spanking, whipping, beating, electrical shocks, cutting, 'pinning and piercing' (infibulation) and humiliation (e.g. being urinated or defecated on, being forced to crawl and bark like a dog or being subjected to verbal abuse).

Some masochistic acts may be dangerous if due care is not taken. 'One particularly dangerous form of Sexual Masochism' according to *DSM-IV*, called 'hypoxyphilia', 'involves sexual arousal by oxygen deprivation obtained by means of chest compression, noose, ligature, plastic bag, mask or chemical ... Accidental deaths sometimes occur.'

Some males with sexual masochism also have fetishism, transvestic fetishism or sexual sadism. Masochistic sexual fantasies are likely to have been present in childhood. The age at which masochistic activities with partners first begin is variable but is commonly reached by early adulthood. Sexual masochism is usually chronic, and the person tends to repeat the same masochistic act. Some individuals may engage in masochistic acts for many years without increasing the potential injuriousness of their acts. Others, however, increase the severity of the masochistic acts over time or during periods of stress, which may eventually result in injury or even death.[10]

6 LEOPOLD VON SACHER-MASOCH

Leopold von Sacher-Masoch was born in 1835 in Lemberg, Galicia, part of the Austrian empire, of Slav, Spanish and Bohemian descent. His father was Chief of Police, and Leopold, as a child, saw brutal prison scenes and fights that left him with deep emotional wounds which troubled him throughout his life. Minority groups, problems of nationality and revolutionary upsurges influenced him. In his work, politics, history, nationalism, eroticism and perversion are all mixed up together. He wrote many distinguished books, all rather unusual, whilst he was a Professor of History at Graz. He used most of his love affairs as material for his writings, such as *The Divorcee* (1865) and later *Venus in Furs* (1870). The latter forms the first part of an unfinished series of novels entitled *The Heritage of Cain*, in which Masoch planned to encompass the themes of war, death, property, money, obsession and love-mastery. Deleuze, in his magisterial book on

Masoch and masochism, enlightens us with his view of the meaning of the *Heritage of Cain*: 'Cain and Christ bear the same pain which leads to the crucifixion of Man',[11] 'who knows no sexual love, no property, no fatherland, no cause, no work: who dies of his own willing, embodying the idea of humanity'.[12] 'Waiting and suspense are essential characteristics of the masochistic experience. Hence the ritual scenes of hanging, crucifixion and other forms of physical suspension in Masoch's novels.'[13] According to Deleuze, Masoch 'has a particular way of desexualizing love and at the same time sexualizing the entire history of humanity'.[14] Masoch's most famous novel, *Venus in Furs*, describes a world of luxury, fantasy, whips, contracts and, of course, furs. Deleuze's brilliant essay 'Coldness and Cruelty' begins by comparing and contrasting the work of de Sade and Masoch, carefully building a case for reinterpreting Masoch's role in our current conception of sadomasochism.

Psychoanalysts have also revealed the overwhelming need for control that masochists exhibit:

The masochist is a revolutionist of self-surrender. The lambskin he wears hides a wolf. His yielding includes defiance, his submissiveness opposition.

Beneath his softness there is hardness; beneath his obsequiousness rebellion is concealed.[15]

Theodor Reik, *Masochism in Modern Man* (1957)

As creator of the performance, the masochist is never truly a victim, because he never really relinquishes control, and in that sense the whole scenario is known to portray only fraudulent suffering.[16]

Robert J. Stoller, *Perversion* (1976)

Masochism seeks only certain specific and individ- ually variable forms of suffering and humiliation. As soon as these reach greater intensity or take a different form they are reacted to with the habitual fear and pain.[17]

R.M. Loewenstein, *A Contribution to the Psychoanalytic Theory of Masochism* (1956)

We see this need for control graphically portrayed in the controversial film *The Piano Teacher* (2001), based on a 1983 novel by the Austrian writer Elfriede Jelinek.

7 THE PIANO TEACHER

The core of this film is the description of a female sadomasochist and her tortured inner world. Erika, the middle-aged daughter, beautifully played by Isobelle Huppert, is a brilliant and talented professor at the Vienna Conservatoire, where she is much respected for her strict, and often callous and virulent attitude towards her students. She lives in a symbiotic relationship of intense hatred and possessiveness with her mother, a woman who has mercilessly suffocated her daughter in a vicarious way for her own lack of fulfilment. In an early scene, Erika retreats to the bathroom away from her mother's invasiveness. She takes a razor blade from her wallet, sits on the edge of the bath, and, carefully looking between her legs with a hand mirror, cuts her genitals. Relief and sexual gratification suffuse her as a trickle of blood stains tub and legs. She then joins mother in the dining room, where she is quickly reprehended for blood running down one of her legs, which is automatically assumed to be the cause of her moodiness – that is, her menstrual period. We are in the 'real female world', where physical/biological signs of femininity are despised and motherhood is shown at its most exploitative and abusive.

But what about relationships with men? Soon we learn that her father is living in an asylum for the mentally ill. Erika has, to some extent, been forced to take his place by sleeping in her mother's bedroom, next to her, both in twin beds. At times she behaves as a caricature of a dysfunctional 'macho' man, frequenting with much bravado a video porn-parlour where she competes with other men to watch hardcore sex scenes. At other times she is the 'peeping Tom' watching unexpected 'victims' in drive-in theatres. On one such occasion, she is caught by one of her indignant victims mid-orgasm while peeing and watching. A polymorphous world of perversion is displayed, first by her sadistic attacks against her own body, and later by her voyeuristic/exhibitionistic conduct. All these lurid aspects of this woman's sexuality take place accompanied by the most beautiful music in the Conservatoire, where she can display her great sense of control in demanding from her students the most exquisite and sensitive performances.

There is an ambiguity about her mental stability; we are left in uncertainty as to whether she has succeeded in creating some balance and peace of mind while engaged in these opposite worlds or if she is on the verge of a breakdown. It is as if her mastery of art and madness is at the core of her existence.

At this point, a young, appealing, handsome and talented man falls for her and becomes her student to be close to her. He is bowled over by this ice maiden, and he is already dreaming of rescuing her from her world of emotional emptiness. It is now, when faced with the possibility of having a loving relationship, that Erika's real psychopathology emerges in full to show her sadomasochistic make-up. A self-destructive dance begins under the deceptive and superficial teasing, bullying and cruel humiliation of this dashing young man. Later on, when he dares to force his way to her home and confronts her mother, he is in possession of a letter she has given to him, which he assumes to be a love letter. Instead, this is a contractual letter in which Erika demands all sorts of cruel and bizarre behaviour involving whips, ropes, chains, wadded-up stockings, a rubber mask and more. Klemmer, the young man, is shocked, to say the least. He responds with complete revulsion and qualifies her as 'mad' and in need of 'treatment'. We are reminded here of the importance of the masochist's contract. Again, Deleuze's insights are illuminating:

We are no longer in the presence of a torturer seizing upon a victim and enjoying her [or him] all the more because she [or he] is unconsenting and unpersuading. We are dealing instead with a victim in search of a torturer and one who needs to educate, persuade and conclude an alliance with the torturer in order to realize the strangest of schemes.[18]

Whereas the sadist is in need of institutions, the masochist is in need of contractual relations. For the masochist, everything must be carefully planned and agreed upon before its achievement. Whereas the sadist is an 'instructor', the masochist is an 'educator'.

This is an extraordinary film which poignantly depicts a world of immense potential for intense beauty combined with the savagery of tremendous waste, destructiveness and the eventual corruption of all those involved.

8 SOME PSYCHODYNAMICS BEHIND THE SCENES

A previous history of some terrible inflicted suffering is usually found in adults who get involved in acts of violence directed either against themselves or against others. The clearest picture derives from the writings of the American psychoanalyst Professor Robert Stoller, who in 1985 conceptualised sadomasochism, or 'S&M' as he and others commonly refer to it, as an attempt to master early trauma by reliving its contents under controlled and safe circumstances. There is an unconscious mechanism at work in that they are unwittingly participating, either actively or passively, in some sort of familiar scenario. In other words, the practitioners of sadomasochism are utterly unaware that this pattern represents some sort of re-enactment of a previous trauma. Its constant repetition is associated with an attempt on their part to resolve the original trauma. When babies or young children were subjected to emotional or physical pain, they were unable to protect themselves or to fend off their attackers because of their lack of physical, let alone emotional, resources. As babies grow to adulthood, they may experience, at times in a compulsive way, the need to repeat these destructive actions. They do not know what causes this compulsion, and most times they are baffled about this. Moreover, they are not aware of any direct or linear links that they can work out in a conscious way in order to get to know what makes them do what they do. To complicate matters further, the original trauma may have been so severe that it was blocked off altogether from consciousness. The fact that there is no conscious recollection is not to say that this has been forgotten for ever. As a matter of fact, it may have been deeply ingrained in another part of the psychic system. Suddenly and unexpectedly, this unresolved, although buried, injury may emerge in the need to engage in risky, seemingly 'irrational' acting out. For example, some individuals become violent as a way of dealing with emotional or physical injuries done to themselves when they were little babies. So, from having been early victims, they could easily become victimisers either of themselves or of others. A role reversal is in operation. They do not feel free: they feel as if 'pushed' from within to repeat some bizarre act. Others experience a need to inflict pain upon themselves, sometimes in such a concealed way that they can easily make their medical practitioners fail to recognise the real core of the problem, and in this way ensure that no appropriate help is found for them.

This was the case with Patricia, a victim of paternal incest, who was referred for psychological treatment by her GP at the age of 36, when, for the first time in her life, she admitted to herself, and then to him, her repressed or 'forgotten' history of incest. Though her GP was an experienced doctor, he had for 15 years felt puzzled at not being able to understand the causes for her extensive and serious psychosomatic complaints, for which she demanded all sorts of surgical interventions. It was fortunate that he did not collude with these requests, which eventually made it possible for her to disclose her participation in incestuous experiences, after 15 years of complete denial. In her mind, she had effectively repressed the memory of sexual abuse, but her body had never forgotten about it. This body became a reminder of her sexual abuse, demanding a radical treatment or harsh punishment as a re-enactment of the early trauma.

Other individuals present their emotional disturbances of self-abuse in more obvious ways, such as in self-burning, cutting, eating disorders or drug abuse. Pain, cutting, and self-harm, including suicidal gestures, are all attempts at repairing the cohesiveness of the self in the face of overwhelming anxiety associated with intense fears of annihilation and the dissolution of the self. Some people in severe distress put their bodies at high risk, subjecting them to controlled mutilation, because, in so doing, they feel in charge. The pain which they experience helps them to conquer their ongoing annihilatory and nihilistic fears.

Frequently, the main symptom is accompanied by some exhibitionistic traits. For example, when these troubled people come to the consulting room, they seem to display their self-inflicted wounds rather deliberately, and with some bravura, to which the clinicians respond with shock and some initial disbelief. In wards of hospitalised female patients suffering from severe anorexia nervosa, it is not unusual to find the display, or shall I say the 'flashing', of their naked, emaciated bodies, which causes much concern and alarm to anyone who happens to be on the wards. This open display of self-inflicted wounds or naked bodies functions as an emotional assault on the unprepared recipients, rapidly turning a masochistic approach into a sadistic one. In other words, in these particular cases they seem to embody both masochism directed towards their own bodies and sadism towards the onlookers.

9 S&M CLUB SCENES

The association of masochism and sadism takes me back to a patient I saw many years ago who used to involve himself in many serious masochistic acts. This man exposed himself to much self-inflicted bodily suffering, concentrating on his genitals as the preferential area for the pain. He began to be aware of an added sense of excitement if this humiliation, a sort of symbolic castration, was performed in public. He became a member of an S&M club with the aim of entering contests, and in this way entertaining a captive and captivated audience. This particular club specialised in the competition for couples to display sadomasochistic acts. The person who inflicted the most pain on his or her partner would become the winner. This man told me very excitedly that he had just been in one of these competitions and had almost won. He described to me a scene which struck me as quite horrific. He was naked on the stage when his partner for the night, a dominatrix, proceeded to inject anaesthetic into his genitalia, using an enormous syringe. Later, the dominatrix sewed up his testicles and scrotum with a very thick needle, making a flap to cover his penis. He experienced an excruciating, 'divine' pain, but he considered it to be negligible since it was quickly superseded by a tremendous sense of sexual frenzy. This escalated even further when he became aware that 400 people were in the audience, some friends and some strangers, reacting with shock. He was the sole object of attraction, the 'star' of the show; all lights were turned in the direction of his genitalia. In a rather naïve way, due to my own lack of clinical experience at the time, I asked whether he had won the contest. Of course not, he answered me in an offended way, and he then explained to me in a rather endearing way that if there were to be a winner it would have been the dominatrix. Due to my lack of clinical experience, I didn't realise that a masochist would ever be rewarded!

I considered this man to be at high risk of further self-destructive actions, but as soon as he became aware of my concern, he strongly denied any suffering. This patient came to see me two or three times, and he eventually decided not to come any longer. In a rather petulant manner, he told me that since he had got to know many of the people in this milieu, he had come to realise that this behaviour was just an 'alternative' normal practice. By now he had access not only to clubs but also to the private homes of 'professionals like yourself' where these acts of sexual sadism in groups and the continual change of partners were the usual practice. He also claimed that he was experiencing a great sense of both elation and internal freedom for the first time in his life.

10 IS SADOMASOCHISM A PERVERSION?

Is the above example a perversion, or 'a profound expression of the desire for self-creation' as Carlo Strenger has hypothesised?[19] Strenger, a Swiss psychoanalyst living in Israel, refuses to relegate this phenomenon to pathological categories that must be diagnosed and cured, and he invites clinicians to make an attempt to gain a deeper understanding of the experience behind it. He himself draws upon the life and philosophical writings of the French author Michel Foucault in an effort to understand, and not just to categorise, one of his female patients as a practitioner of severe sadomasochism. Foucault, a loyal follower of the Marquis de Sade, is also an extreme writer who describes society and its contradictions. He shares with de Sade terrified images of incarceration throughout his life.

Foucault was deeply fascinated with the world of consensual S&M. During the 1970s, he immersed himself in the world of S&M by visiting the gay scene in California. Although he refused to acknowledge his own emotional pain, he was not without memories, as the autobiographical material in his writings shows. On one occasion, Foucault had been forced by his father to watch a physical amputation. Strenger wonders:

What went through the child's mind when he underwent this mindless act of cruelty? His father was a doctor and Michel must have felt endangered by a father who was so insensitive to his son's psyche, particularly because he must have assumed that his father himself cut limbs off people.

This reminded me of a scene in *The Sopranos*, the American Mafia television soap, in which Tony, the main character, while mutilating one of his own associates, experiences a flashback scene in which his father, a butcher, cuts off the arms of somebody who had refused to comply with his blackmail threats. The relation to castration anxiety is unavoidable.

Returning to my previous patient, his early history was characterised by the most terrible and deprived background. He had been subjected to much suffering and abuse, from which he had been incapable of defending himself. He was unable to look at the connection between the unbearable pain of the past and his present predicament. Instead, he had created for himself a belief in his own freedom by virtue of being an 'active' participant in the inflicted pain. It was more manageable for him to go on repeating these experiences over which he had a degree of control, rather than go through the process of psychotherapy into the unknown picture of the extreme emotional suffering in his own life. The need to be watched or witnessed by others – the accompanying voyeuristic and exhibitionistic features – is often present in people who have themselves, as children, been witnesses of domestic violence. They become, now, the leading actors in an open arena, displaying their emotional pain in a systematic and organised way, and in a manic fashion.

But are we, the psychotherapists, not just simplifying extremely complex phenomena in all-too- easy pathologising and categorising, in order to cover up our own sense of inadequacy at not really understanding what is going on in the inner lives of these people? Certainly S&M practices appear to be futile attempts to cover up old, but still open, wounds. The problem is that we wonder whether we can honestly declare that we are able to accompany that individual into looking at the intricacies of his being, without being shaken by the intense pain of not being able to fully understand him or her. But we have to talk about our pain, the pain that we as clinicians experience when capable of admitting that we can feel confused and helpless in our quest to understand and 'cure' all ailments. Are these individuals making the right decision when refusing treatment, since this will only intensify the pain even more in a non-controlled way? Are our patients allowed from within to engage in a therapeutic quest where emotional suffering will replace the physically sexualised suffering? We know that any attempt at a quick, sharp treatment is out of question. Such quick treatments would serve only to foster a repetition of their acting-out.

11 DENIAL AND DISASTER IN SADOMASOCHISM

You're trying to make out that I just went out and blatantly killed somebody ... [that] nobody went through hell. Enjoyment turned to disaster.[20]

Fred West

Throughout the course of my clinical work with individuals who engage in sadomasochistic acts, I have frequently observed a strong sense of denial. Overtly sadomasochistic people refuse to admit to any adverse consequences, either physical or emotional, that their actions may cause to others involved in these activities. Only in some intractable cases of paedophilia have I encountered the same defensive mechanism to such a degree. Sadomasochists adamantly claim that not only they but also the other individuals involved experience a sense of freedom in that they choose what they 'want' to do. This sense of freedom is emphasised not only internally but also externally – particularly in relation to the ostensibly consensual nature of the activities. It is important to remember that dehumanisation, the commonest feature of the perversions, is also present in S&M. Erich Fromm in *The Heart of Man* (1964) poignantly links dehumanisation and freedom when describing the aim of sadism as the need 'to transform a man into a thing, something animate into something inanimate, since by complete and absolute control the living loses one essential quality of life – freedom'.[21]

A frequent finding in perversions is that the individual is aware of 'being taken over' and attempts to fight his or her perverse action but usually fails and so succumbs to the action. Afterwards, he or she experiences overwhelming shame, self-disgust and depression. So there is a repetitive cycle in which the person afflicted by a perversion succumbs to the action, in order to be relieved of a powerful sense of sexual anxiety, only to return to the previous predicament of increasing sexual anxiety, which, after being assuaged in the short- term, once more demands the execution of the same bizarre and 'illogical' act.[22] Alongside the repetitive cycle of shame, self-disgust and depression exists an unconscious desire to humiliate or hurt another person. In sadomasochism there is a denial of this recognised cycle of feelings.

The alleged 'consensual' nature of sadomasochism reinforces a lack of motivation for change that makes it difficult to reach the individual in any therapeutic way. It effectively interferes with the possibility of seeking professional help or of undergoing therapy. Only a few ever come for professional help, and, if they do, these people usually shy away from therapy on the grounds that there is no need for it, because each sadomasochist is supposedly acting out of mutual consent.

In sadomasochism this 'contractual agreement' between the parties concerned forms the pivotal point of a system in which control-taking is the most important ingredient. Both parties share the control, and role reversal is present – but only with the tacit agreement of the other(s). The illusion of being in complete control is essential.

At times, fatal accidents can occur. Let us illustrate this sad situation with a clinical example. A heterosexual couple together devised an intricate and convoluted 'game'. In bed, the woman would be chained, and the man would begin to suffocate her with a silk scarf (incidentally, the only present his mother had ever given her). When she felt herself to be on the very edge of being unable to breathe at all, he would suddenly loosen the strangulation knot and let her free. Both would reach simultaneous orgasm. For a successful conclusion, intense eye contact was required throughout the whole exercise as this demonstrated their mutual trust. On one occasion, the man could not stop himself, despite his claim that he wanted to do so. He was unable to 'let it go' because he 'saw' and 'sensed' in her eyes that she was terrified. He was struck by what he experienced as this lack of trust on her part, which precipitated him to 'lose it altogether' and so cause her 'accidental death'. He was utterly devastated by her death and attended all the court proceedings in a state of deep depression. He was unable to believe that he had actually *killed* her. This also illustrates an important point, namely that sadomasochistic actions like this, per- formed by 'mutual consent' between two parties, are compulsive and repetitive and therefore always require the other partner's survival. Death, whenever it occurs, is almost always accidental since this is an outcome that has never consciously entered their minds. The surviving, disbelieving partner invariably proclaims, 'it was just a game', full of anguish and distress.

12 SIMILARITIES AND DIFFERENCES IN SADOMASOCHISM AND DOMESTIC VIOLENCE

In the light of these cases, I think it is significant to link sadomasochistic behaviour with domestic violence, in which control and safety are usually absent. An important sociocultural phenomenon is the gender-associated expression of basic emotions, such as anger or crying. In other words, they are 'gender prescribed or proscribed'.[23] For example, men are encouraged to show anger, because it is associated with being in charge, being in authority and with being self-assertive. Women are inhibited from showing anger, which would turn away their male lovers, and encouraged to cry, because by so doing they show vulnerability, frailty and weakness – and in this way can get anything they want from their men. There is a new fashion to encourage men to cry, but I doubt if a similar encouragement in women to express anger would elicit such a welcome response. On the contrary, as soon as women shout or show their anger in any way, men are ready to flee. The woman and mother who feels unable to express her frustration, impotence and helplessness, because she knows that her male partner will run away from her, may seem to have no other alternative but to take out such negative feelings on her children, who are completely at her mercy; that is to say, the only people to whom she can show her anger and who cannot run away are her children.[24] This could be the first step in a cycle of physical or sexual abuse. Another option for women is to turn their anger inwards, which induces greater depression, and to harbour dreams of revenge. Women experience a losing battle if they show a negative response by demonstrating annoyance or irritation, particularly if this is coupled with abuse of power or a controlling attitude, which is neither expected from them nor condoned.

It is likely that young women who have experienced early emotional deprivation, and who have failed to learn self-assertion during adolescence, will become increasingly dissatisfied with them- selves and their own bodies. This is often manifest during adolescence in the form of eating disorders, such as anorexia and bulimia, promiscuity, drug abuse, self-cutting and burning. These are the pre- cursors of abusive behaviour to others and constitute part of the psychological profile of the female abuser. The ambivalence towards the female body, and towards mother, lies at the heart of the cycle of abuse. As they grow older, they may find enormous internal difficulties in achieving healthy, satisfactory, mature emotional relationships. Instead, a young woman might easily enter relationships with men or other women with whom a sadomasochistic pattern emerges. It is extremely difficult for these women to extricate themselves from these relationships. In fact, when and if they do manage to give them up, they do so only in order to start a new relationship, which in no time acquires the same characteristics as the previous one. This is because the brutish partner represents an internal part of herself, the partner becoming the embodiment of her own self-hate. She might now no longer need to attack her own body in different ways because her partner has been unconsciously assigned to perform this role. Heterosexual intercourse with sadistic characteristics becomes the rule. Though on the surface the woman is submissive, compliant and passive, revenge is being harboured in different daydreams, dreams and fantasies. Often, dreams of a pregnancy are engendered with different connotations, for example to fall pregnant as an expression of revenge against the man who is so undermining and contemptuous. Or, if left alone, feeling isolated and despondent, the young woman might want to have a child to keep her company and to provide her with unconditional affection. She is quite unaware that, left to her own devices, she may easily fall into abusive actions against her baby, since she is unable, psychologically and otherwise, to deliver all that is required from a 'good enough' mother. Those who equate motherhood with healthy and mature development do not usually assume such motivations.

Domestic violence can escalate to the point where all family members become involved and affected, to a greater or lesser degree. The most frequent sociological example is that of a man who feels undermined and frustrated, and who acts out against his wife, with the result that their children are at the mercy of his violent acts and become terrified at the fear of their parent's eventual death at the hands of the partner. When he goes to work, the husband or stepfather leaves behind a pained and battered wife, who is now in control of the domestic sphere. Though her domestic duties may afford her no small amount of power and responsibility, it is often an unsatisfying power, linked as it is to isolation from outside society and dependence on the husband. It is then that the woman identifies with the aggressor (her male partner) and works out her own aggression against her child, who in turn becomes the weak family member and the 'appropriate' target for the expression of hostility, aggression and, sometimes, sexualised violence. This outcome is different from the sadomasochistic situations in which the script is a fixed one, requiring the safety of a well-established framework.

13 REPETITION COMPULSION AND THE BODY AS THE TORTURER

Clinically I have encountered many women suffering from severe psychopathology, associated with an internal impulse, which often becomes trans- formed into a 'need' to harm their own children. This is the result of both acute and cumulative sexual traumas inflicted on them by both parents.

McDougall tells us in *Theatres of the Body* that 'The body, like the mind, is subject to the repetition compulsion', and she also reminds us that 'Freud in *Beyond the Pleasure Principle* linked this manifestation to destructive impulses and also an attempt to manage trauma.'[25]

Ethel Person has produced a rich and comprehensive study of the various sadomasochistic fantasies in women, including beating, and she has coined the term 'the body silenced' (meaning the lack of sexual desire) and 'the body as the enemy' (meaning hypochondriacal symptoms). Following this, I believe a fitting term for many of my female patients' specific predicaments could be 'the body as the torturer'.[26] This would signal the compulsive urges these women experience, unconsciously making their bodies function as an effective torture tool that will lead them to become victimisers of themselves and of their babies. As already mentioned, at times a partner becomes unconsciously designated as the torturer, representing an internal part of herself.

Denial, a defence mechanism often utilised in those suffering from severe and repeated traumas, is used for avoiding 'the black hole' – in other words, the dread of emptiness, which is represented by 'absence'. (Since the mental representation of being wanted and/or desired was never present, we are unable to talk about a sense of loss.) Repeated traumas of rejection are turned into a chronic, masked depression, linked to experiences of deprivation, neglect and abuse. Faced with such trauma, individuals use denial as a mechanism of defence in order to ward off psychic pain. Every form of risk-taking could be construed as a manic defence. Paradoxically, people often place themselves in painful, life-threatening, masochistic situations to achieve psychological survival. Because of all the risks involved, this reassures them that they are still alive. Life-threatening behaviours are used as a 'survival minikit'.[27]

I have also encountered women who have applied the most painful and dangerous practices to their bodies as a means to control their mounting desires to attack their own offspring. They also admit to sexual gratification achieved through these practices.

This 'perverse solution' becomes an intergenerational legacy, which can be carried through many future generations if not properly understood. This again is an example of a compulsion to repeat, which returns us to the original trauma. Repeated pregnancies may be an example of this. Perhaps it is easier to see such a cycle of victim– perpetrator interactions more easily in other types of abuse rather than in the repetition of falling pregnant.

14 MALIGNANT BONDING

Under normal circumstances, adults develop close partnerships in later years which allow for a continuous sense of intimacy. This includes a degree of sadomasochism, tolerated because of the security generated by the long-term relationship. Such a relationship is endowed with both sexual gratification, which provides stability, and mutual trust, so enabling the couple to cope with daily stresses. However, some couples are not able to achieve such intimacy, and the stress can either lead to enmeshment, whereby the two of them feel stuck together, or to alienation from one another. Such a relationship will oscillate between these two states, and the same pattern may eventually extend to their offspring.

Families appearing in court cases are often at the severe end of the spectrum of personality difficulties and illustrate how impaired ability to form relationships can frequently lead to a 'malignant bonding' between two adults. This happens when both parents have insecure attachments and unresolved traumas; they feel insecure and function with impaired or immature object relations. A priori, they have mated because of this mutual immaturity, and their own interdependence is doomed to fail with the arrival of a baby, which is experienced, unconsciously, as a continuous threat to the relationship. Paradoxically, the child becomes the excuse for an increasing interdependence between mother and father, which exacerbates their alienation from the child, who becomes, therefore, a projective bad object. The child is 'used' within a symbiotic relationship (i.e. not as a separate person with needs) and is both sexually abused and then abandoned.

Such bonding serves to 'stabilise' the mental functioning of both parents within their relation-ship in a perverse way. Both parents project their sadistic needs onto a third person who is felt to be vulnerable. For example, the West case demonstrates an almost unprecedented situation of violence, rape and killing, all found out almost by chance. In so many newspaper accounts, Fred West had been cast as the unemotional man who forced his wife Rose to practice prostitution so that he might watch her perform with other men. But Rose

West acted as accomplice to her husband in the sexual assault and eventual killing of a great number of young women – including their own daughters.

A patient of mine had a history that included a development of acts initially directed against herself, such as self-cutting, drinking and the unconscious seeking out of severe sadomasochistic relationships. These, she used for her own perpetuation as a victim and also as a survivor. Later, she added to her long list of self-inflicted punishment that of having babies – who, because of her apparent lack of concern and proper care, were subsequently taken away from her. This course of action appeared to be a masochistic quest for more severe punishment by a sadistic and erratic part of her mind chasing her indiscriminately as a woman and as a mother. She was obviously unaware of the links between her early abuse and her 'addiction' to sadomasochistic relationships. Finally, in a feeble attempt to be in control of a relationship, she associated herself with a minor and got impregnated by him, having seduced him with the appealing thought of becoming a father at the tender age of 14. In the first instance, it may appear that she was successful in the creation of a role reversal that cast her as the perpetrator and the minor as the victim. This was not so; on the contrary, once more she became the victim when the 14-year-old boy, with the help of his family, led a humiliating and mocking campaign against her which caused her to have her baby taken away from birth.

The girl had a horrendous early life history, which included all sorts of emotional, physical and sexual abuse. Both her parents had been engaged in a sort of 'malignant bonding', becoming united 'parents' in cruel and sadistic attacks on their daughter, which included using her for pornographic purposes and later for prostitution; these incidents of abuse were accompanied by the infliction of physical pain, with horrific sexual connotations. It goes without saying that the cases of Fred and Rose West, and Ian Brady and Myra Hindley are extreme examples of malignant bonding.

15 MOTHERS AS CREATORS OF SADOMASOCHISM

Imre Hermann was the first psychoanalyst to observe and record sadomasochistic phenomena in the mother–child relationship in his important paper 'Clinging-Going in-Search' (1976).[28] This concept was later further explored and expanded by Mervin Glasser (1979)[29] in his well-known conception of the 'core- complex'. However Glasser never acknowledged Hermann's work, or his original findings.

After years of clinical experience, I have had to acknowledge that female perversion does exist, though the mental mechanisms are different from those found in men. Proper acknowledgement of the possibility of female perversion was absent because motherhood had been widely glorified to the extent of equating the achievement of motherhood with good mental health. It had been wrongly assumed that women who become mothers feel free of conflict and totally fulfilled.

Women commit their perverse actions against themselves or what they regard as an extension of themselves, their babies.[30] Without this insight, a good deal of the treatment of women has been based on the false premise that what applies to male sadomasochism applies equally to female sadomasochism. A significant percentage of the patients we see (and this refers to both men and women) are themselves the victims of sexual abuse as children. Furthermore, the histories of children almost invariably include an early psycho-pathology of self-abuse and/or sadomasochistic relationships.

Expressing her struggle against the urge to abuse her child, a woman wrote:

My feelings of arousal in certain situations with O., my 18 month old son, started a couple of weeks ago. I have touched him twice in response to those feelings. After having spoken to my husband, the Psychiatric Social Worker, and the NSPCC, I have been jolted out of it. I now recognize when I am aroused but I will not act on those feelings inappropriately. When he is toddling around I feel that he is my son, my baby and I love him as such. I would not hurt him physically and I do not want to hurt him psychologically either. I have a daughter, my feelings for her have always been those of a loving mother-daughter relationship.

It may sound odd, but motherhood provides an excellent vehicle for some women to exercise perverse and perverting attitudes towards their offspring, and also retaliation against their own mothers, through sadomasochistic practices. Becoming a mother is a difficult and complex task which demands much from women, and the rewards may not be immediately apparent – especially to those whose mothering abilities have been impaired by early deprivations and constant abuse.

A pregnancy at an early age often coincides with the precise age of the woman's own mother's pregnancy. Pregnancy as an outcome of a sense of inadequacy, hatred or revenge (conscious or unconscious), or a 'quick replacement' pregnancy, can also lead to mothering disorders. It is not infrequent to find a 'quick replacement' pregnancy in some women, following an incident of miscarriage, stillbirth or cot death. The unexpected and sudden loss of a baby can lead to a new pregnancy in an attempt to prevent these mothers from mourning the lost child. This is thought to be a hidden predisposing factor towards child abuse. The dead baby is the perfect one; the replacement is the flawed one. Some mothers who find themselves in this particular predicament of not being able to mourn, coupled with the demands of the newly born baby, will abuse the new infant. In addition, a lack of emotional and practical resources during pregnancy and early mothering is also a factor leading to poor mothering, as are continuing relationships of an uncaring, violent or sadomasochistic nature.

The origins of this disturbance could go back as early as the woman's own birth, if her gender was not welcomed by her family or was even a source of great disappointment. Obviously, this will seriously affect the relationship between the mother and her baby.

In contrast to the above, an article that appeared in the *Independent* on 15 October 1993 – 'Child Murderer Confesses at Last' – describes how the 24-year-old nurse Beverley Allit admitted to having killed four children and attacked nine others, all of them on her ward and under her care. It is a short piece on the first page in a serious paper. It is noted, 'at her trial she was suffering from anorexia nervosa ... Allit had been inflicting serious injury on her own body while a student nurse.' A Home Office forensic psychiatrist described her as 'this very damaged lady'.

As we can see in the newspaper account, the history of Beverly Allit contained horrific incidents of self-mutilation during her years as a student nurse. Had this new concept of female perversion and the profile of the female abuser been taken into account, then a job involving 'mothering' duties for someone who has an early history of self-abuse would at least have been discouraged, and it might not have been pursued. It is this misassessment that has led to some very 'damaged ladies' being so misunderstood as to be denied the treatment they need, and for which they sometimes plead. Such attitudes are among the reasons why it is taking so long for the profession, not to mention the public, to accept that women as mothers or in mothering professions can inflict irreparable dam- age on the children for whom they are supposed to care.

These are only two examples of female abuse, one involving intrafamilial sexual abuse and the other, murderous violence towards children in a residential setting. This is not indeed the only difference. The first woman asked for professional help when she felt incapable of dealing adequately with her role as mother to her youngest child. The abusive activity of the other woman was found out only after a considerable period of time, during which she had been working in one of the 'caring' professions and inflicting severe physical harm to several children placed under her care.

It would be possible to enunciate many more differences, but my aim is to point out the blatant similarity present in both cases, in that nobody, over a long period of time, was able to suspect anything wrong with either of the two women. The first case concerns the domestic sphere, involving husband, grandparents and other children. Even when the woman asked for help, she still had to refer herself for psychiatric assessment. This is a very different outcome from what would have happened in a similar situation to her male counterpart. The other case implicated all sorts of co-workers who had known the woman at different stages of her professional development: training as a nurse, being successful at applying for a job taking care of small children, working daily together. My assumption based on my clinical findings is that both women have experienced much psychic pain because of their own abusive behaviour.

16 QUESTIONS OF DANGEROUSNESS

Being a woman may not fit in with our perception of a serial killer – which, of course, she is. In fact, if we keep in mind this particular female psychopathology it may be easier to predict dangerousness in a woman than in a man. The actual dangerousness in the Beverley Allit case is devastatingly obvious. But what determines these horrific killings? What has been overlooked or even neglected? Could this violent behaviour have been predicted at an earlier stage? Obviously, some circumstances are bound to increase female dangerousness. But may we talk of this dangerousness as being intrinsically female? We must consider carefully how to use this awful experience to learn of possible ways to improve our detection and assessment of such danger in order to prevent further criminal behaviour in the future.

Are we capable of recognising these specific problems? Can we assess dangerousness and risk circumstances in such a way as to establish patterns which could act as indicators of future dangerous behaviour, or the situations in which hostility and aggression could easily be triggered off?

These powers of assessment are unequally distributed. Women have control of the domestic sphere where abuse is hidden away, whereas men have access to public power where transgressions are in the open with the 'natural' concomitant of humiliation and punishment being the available resources.

The outcome of this gender split affects individuals and society in general since women are to be seen as victims, being treated with sedatives. Men are seen invariably as perpetrators, faced with 'penalisation' and punishment. This leads to the continuation of seeing women as victims, who are never allowed to disclose their dreams of revenge, or to show abuse of power and their extreme need to be in control.

17 AN ATTEMPT TO UNDERSTAND THE 'UNTHINKABLE'

The most notorious case of extra-familial abuse by a couple was that of Ian Brady with Myra Hindley. It seems that Ian Brady was familiar with the Marquis de Sade's writings and particularly with his dictum that 'cruelty is one of the most natural human feelings, one of the sweetest of man's inclinations, one of the most intense he has received from nature'. According to Brian Masters, Ian Brady would 'gain succour from his assertion that murder was also in the natural order of things'.[31]

The West case, which occurred two decades after the Ian Brady–Myra Hindley case, challenged even further our capacity to think – let alone to under- stand the plethora of extraordinary, abhorrent mental processes, made even worse due to the malignant bonding between mother and father, that could lead to their combined action against their own children and others'.

The temptation with someone like Rosemary West is to demonise the offender, characterising her as a monstrous aberration bearing no relation to the rest of humanity, let alone womanhood. The sheer horror at the evidence recounted in this case left most people shocked and bewildered. Even for those of us working in the field of psychiatry, there is much that is inexplicable in this relationship between a man and woman, which involved sexual perversion, incest, killing and mutilation. How- ever, one aspect that may well be neglected and ignored is that of female domestic sexual abuse, of which Rosemary West is an extreme example. Apart from the phenomenon of battering babies, which is now well known, other predicaments associated with motherhood have been ignored or undiagnosed hitherto. The stereotyped view that 'women are victims and men abusers' has been a socially accepted formula. Female sexual abuse is largely ignored and denied by women's groups because it fits uncomfortably with the idea of women as the exploited sex. Yet, it is the very fact that women have been abused that can lead them in turn to abusive behaviour. Perversion of mother- hood is invariably the end product of serial abuse or chronic infantile neglect. This condition involves at least three generations in which faulty and inadequate mothering perpetuates itself in a circular motion, each successive generation renewing the cycle of abuse.

18 TREATMENT IMPLICATIONS

The reason for the compulsive need in individuals to repeat abusing actions against themselves and others cannot easily be provided, but it is usually linked to avoidance of mourning, lack of symbolic functioning and persecutory guilt. It is the belief of those who work with psychoanalytic methods that the only way to obtain long-term internal changes is through psychoanalytical psychotherapy, which will provide a psychological understanding of the self-inflicted behaviour. We also know that the dynamics of sadomasochism make a therapeutic alliance, almost by definition, a contradiction in terms since dynamic psychotherapy requires painful emotional self-examination for the gaining of insight – contrary to the sadomasochist's well- known acting out practices, which are far less threatening to them since they are so deeply ingrained. Psychoanalysts may also have to face the risk that the emotional pain of therapy will be corrupted into masochistic gratification.

A few years ago, I received the following self-referral from a woman in great need of therapy:

I am writing to you in desperation. I need help. I am a 26-year-old woman, with six children presently in care and one due, within the next few weeks, which it also looks as though I am going to lose. I desperately want my children back, but also recognized that I'm in this position because of my own abuse as a child. One of my daughters was sexually abused by one of my abusers. I am now experiencing flashbacks, nightmares, and awful depression. I can't bear to be touched by my partner – I also recognize that my relationship is very brutal. I don't want it anymore. P.S. I was sexually abused by 5 different people from the age of 2–12 years, and then raped at the age of 17 years. My mother was physically abusing me at this time too.

This letter was from a woman who had been charged with aiding and abetting sexual abuse. She had taken her daughter to be babysat by her own stepfather, who had previously abused her as a child. A high degree of unconscious identification with her own daughter is present. Also present is a sense of self-loathing confirmed by her sadomasochistic relations and brutal treatment of her own body. This constitutes yet another category in which the abuse is simultaneously active and unconscious. In other words, she is quite unaware of her participation in a cycle in which she is perpetuating her own trauma by placing her child in identical circumstances to those she suffered, because the original trauma – her own abuse and the complex mix of feelings it engendered – had been buried away, and only emerged into consciousness when she herself became aware of her own daughter's abuse.

She was placed in a therapeutic group, and only there was she able to look into her own 'abusing' behaviour, when supported by others with similar histories. There was no chance for her to feel judged by others. On the contrary, she experienced this constant confrontation of 'taking in' her own sense of responsibility as enlightening and ext-remely helpful. In turn, her own capacity for internal and constant change provided the others with reassurance about their own capacity to give positive things. Much cohesiveness, connectedness and mutuality emerged in the group affiliation.

Group psychotherapy offers particular

advantages, as a treatment option, for victims and perpetrators of sexual abuse, since secrecy and isolation are replaced by disclosure within the contained atmosphere of the group.[32] People confront past pain and abuse, and become aware of their need for revenge, a need that fuels their capacity for perpetrating abuse in their turn. Yet it remains a sad fact that, while the treatment of victims is encouraged and everyone is rightly concerned about their welfare, the same does not apply to the offenders, who are believed to be the products of 'evil forces'.

A degree of sadism and masochism is present in all sexual relationships. While cases like that of Fred and Rosemary West are at the extreme end of this psychological spectrum, bearing only minimal resemblance to the abuse of which I have been writing, many other cases do involve people who need, and can be given, help. To use simplistic moral judgements is not helpful in furthering understanding and reflects more on the one making the judgement than the one being judged. Sadomasochistic rituals and behaviour are a solution, of sorts, to unbearable psychic pain. They may give immense pleasure to those who practice them, but at a cost of real intimacy and with the potential for real damage to others. The much vaunted sense of freedom to which the sadomasochist attests is belied by the overwhelming need for control and the endless repetition of the same scenarios. In avoiding the anxiety and trauma that dominates their being, they are destined to repeat it. The seeds of future sadomasochism, whether the consensual games of the S&M club scene or the malignant bonding of the serial abuser, are formed in early childhood. More adequate resources should be made available to provide appropriately for mothers and babies, and for mothers to escape abusive partners, so that these people may achieve some understanding of their inner lives. Only with public awareness of these traumatic problems can we start to break the cycles of abuse that secrecy and the fear of public humiliation encourage.

19 THE INSTITUTIONALIZATION OF PERVERSION

The Political Torturer: a suitable case for treatment?

We might reach a better understanding of the actions of torturers and of other agents of repressive regimes if we analyze the similarities and differences between their actions and those of patients who suffer from perversions

There is a difference between lay and psychoanalytical language over the term "perversion". Whereas ordinarily the word is pejorative and carries moral implications, in psychoanalytic language it refers to a dysfunction of the sexual component of personality development. Social structures and cultural environments play a part in this, alongside biological and psychological factors.

It may be useful to examine the psychodynamics

of the "torturer" and more generally of the "repressor" sanctioned by "state terrorism" that condones systematic violations of law and human rights by those in power. As citizens of the world this is obviously an area of great concern to us all.

I will speculate about the treatability or non-treatability of individuals who have committed acts of torture and later found themselves seeking professional help to deal with emerging symptoms. Such symptoms might involve either no longer being able to find an easy release (libidinal discharge) for their "learned" or "gained" sadism, or most often unbearable guilt regarding their past activities. This approach is especially poignant and relevant in my home country, Argentina, which has always had a large population of psychoanalysts, and where psychodynamic thinking has enjoyed a long and populist tradition. During the Dirty War, the psychoanalytical profession was an important target for the State's persecution and terrorization, and many practitioners were secretly arrested and subjected to torture, and they, and members of their families, were among the "desaparecidos".

Through this I became aware of the dilemmas that could emerge from the practice of psychodynamic psychotherapy under a repressive regime or dictatorship.

In dictatorships it is common for psychoanalysis as a field of study and transaction to become the object of persecution since its key objective is the liberation of individuals. I am indebted to Janine Puget's work in this area and her concept of 'the overlapping worlds'[33].

The Repressive System

Usually repressive actions or torture enacted under an organized, fully legalized system endorsed by the State are not seen as perverse. The repressive State encourages perversion on a collective and organized level by creating a scale of rewards for perverse actions. A distinction is established between the perverse dynamics sanctioned by the State, and the behaviour of the habitually perverse individual.

We cannot fully understand the actions of the torturer and the motivation for them without understanding the character of the state whose agent he is. The repressive state is typically not a democracy. It takes the view that citizens exist to protect the state rather than the other way around. Therefore, the state is justified in acting against individuals that fail to protect it. Such citizens are subversive, and those who actively work against the government are enemies of the state. The definition of treason is harsh, but relatively clear. The definition of subversion on the other hand is arbitrary, and capricious, likely to change from day to day, and from person to person. Torture is justified as a means to detect subversion, and is usually considered as more necessary to the protection of the state than punishment.

In the minds of the rulers there is no distinction between the government and the state. In their definition disloyalty to the former cannot fail to be disloyalty to the latter. Given that basic attitude, any means necessary are justified for protection of the alleged good of the state (not just its protection from destruction). This is interpreted literally so that "the good of the state" may override the law of the land. At the most fundamental level, whatever the constitution may say, the government is not prepared to contemplate a change of government by peaceful means. If the constitution can be overridden, so can every category of law including those protecting human rights. Yet no government willingly foregoes its claim to legality, so attempts are made by evasion, deception, euphemism, subterfuge and, above all, secrecy, to disguise the fact that the law is being flouted. Nevertheless, the flouters are aware of what they are doing. Thus, deep psychological tensions are built into the repressive state. It is acting for the "good" but knows that its actions are "wrong". This intensifies the need in the minds of the government and its agents to repress and to hurt. It is not too far-fetched to describe the state apparatus that serves such a government as perverse. It is hardly surprising that the agents who constitute the apparatus are condemned, voluntarily or otherwise, to carry out perverse actions. But does that make those individual agents perverts?

The institution of such a system already incorporates elements of perversion, with the inherent need to inflict pain in a sexualized way. In this way, within the upper echelons of the State, the authorities' perverse ideology articulates a disavowal of differentiation. In other words, anyone whose set of interests or ideology is not identical to those in charge of the system is considered to be an "enemy" and his/her thoughts and actions are considered "subversive". Thus, a system of repression is created.

This is a dictatorship, the aim of which becomes

the extermination of the "enemy" and, therefore, sanctioning of the "torturer". No limits are placed on the actions of the torturer in materializing this split, which in itself contains a massive denial of external and psychological reality. As observed earlier, the capriciousness of the "definition" of what is subversive creates ambiguity, confusion and collective fear.

Civil rights are distorted and removed. The population is divided into two: those who are affected; and those who are not. This division is made artificially and randomly by means of arbitrarily repressive actions, increasing ambiguity and confusion, and producing paralysis of action and thought processes.

In spite of the differences that have been sketched out here, one could argue that to speak of the 'Perverse State' under such conditions is completely warranted.

Torture is used first as an instrument to obtain information and subsequently to immobilize opposition to the authorities.

The torturer or executioner is a member of a well-defined hierarchy that compels his obedience and at the same time exonerates him insofar as his actions are the result of following orders especially since failure to obey can result in punishment. Nevertheless, he/she well knows that he is acting against generally accepted social conventions and even against the body of the law. It is characteristic of many of these situations that the normal body of law is left unchanged. Consequently, murder, torture, physical harassment of prisoners and even abducting or "disappearing" them could easily constitute a crime. Therefore a conflict is created between following orders and abiding by the "law".

Thus, the torturer cannot be regarded as only an official following orders, or as a part of a fully, and lawfully, backed element of government action that would separate him completely from the case of the perverse individual. The latter is aware of the antisocial and sometimes criminal traits of his actions. An element of risk-taking and shame is consequently ever-present. In the case of the torturer, this is also partially the case. Not only can he not fully rely on his actions being above ultimate punishment by the State's legal system, but he is continuously conscious of over-reaching the law. The operation in which he is involved is clandestine since people are abducted rather than made legal prisoners. Places of detention are often unknown or, if known, not revealed to the prisoner's relatives.

Thus the torturer is acting far more under his own volition than if he were discharging his duties to the letter of the law.

Similarities and differences between perverse individuals and torturers

Perverse acts are always accompanied by the need to inflict pain. In the case of the perverse individual, this need is an internal one that provides him with sexual gratification, whereas the torturer might "learn" to experience gratification while he fulfills his duty. Perverse patients are usually unaware of causing pain during this process. They experience a sense of shame and guilt about their actions, though these are of different degrees and are not obviously apparent to casual observers. Even professionals sometimes overlook these when they are expecting more overt 'admissions' of guilt from offenders. Often the individual's actions are easily recognised as being harmful to others and society, which indicates a need for a punitive response, i.e. a wish to be detected and caught.

The person who commits the perverse act in any given situation in a democracy is punished by society's legislation, enacted to protect its citizens.

But such perverse actions under autocratic governments are not only organized, sanctioned and the preserve of some individuals, but are also rewarded by official promotion. Under the pretense of caring for citizens' well-being and protecting them from chaos through 'subversion', the State appoints official agents to execute organized, systematic and brutal actions themselves. Deprived of the usual defence procedures, citizens, unarmed and taken into custody, are subjected to painful torture, and systematic degradation in many cases, devoid of any interrogative purpose, solely for the sake of forcing them - and through them the entire population - into total submission to State power.

In this we can observe the presence of the perverse characteristic of the need for control, at play both internally and externally. The perverse individual responds to an inner compulsion to be in control as revenge for earlier experiences of deprivation when he felt neglected and humiliated. The torturer's more apparent need belongs to the external order of the State, and his control, in the context of hierarchy, is illusory.

In both individuals, the sadistic actions - very different from aggression - which inflict pain and terror, are felt to be wrong, but the reasons for sustaining them are different. In the case of the pervert the element of compulsion is present together with the inner knowledge of its being the only way to relieve his mounting sexual anxiety. He is painfully aware of the compulsion to repeat the action, but quite oblivious to the hostility and the symbolism attached to it. Furthermore, he is deeply unconscious of whom he hates and on whom he wants to exact revenge. Typically, he does not understand why this particular, sometimes bizarre, activity that he knows is wrong, which actually provides him with only a short-lived feeling of pleasure and is immediately replaced by shame and disgust, makes him feel better. It is all the more puzzling to him when there are so many options at hand, which obviously could be more satisfactory and safer in his social surroundings.

In developmental terms, the perverse person has been thwarted at an early age from achieving sexual emotional maturity (i.e. genital sexuality), partly as a result of his mother's preventing his process of separation and individuation. This will be responsible, later on, for his difficulties in forming satisfactory relationships, and is crucial to the understanding of perversion. It creates in the perverse individual a deep belief that he is not a whole being, but his mother's part-object. From early on in his life he has felt undesired and ignored, or alternatively a vital but unidentifiable part of his parents' lives (usually his mother's). In the latter case he will feel smothered and 'over-protected', which actually means totally unprotected. Both situations create enormous insecurity and vulnerability in him, and prompt intense hatred towards the culprit and the most important during his early life - his mother.[34] Having been victims, such people become the victimizers.

The torturer, on the other hand, uses sadism consciously as his main aim for his ulterior motives, which have to do with 'working' for a higher structure and being 'good' at his 'job' as well as his belief that his actions will bring well-being to the whole of society. Not only has he been given permission, he is ordered, and paid, to practice perverse actions. The compulsive element so deeply felt by the perverse individual - and which I consider to be the most redeeming and hopeful feature - is missing in the torturer, who is obeying orders from above. The torturer is provided with his victims whereas the perverse individual chooses them. In both cases, a particular psychopathology is in operation in which victims of both groups are experienced to be part-objects of perverse designs. In both cases sexualization of the sadistic bodily attacks is the rule. In the perverse individual the sexualization is a defence against depression and it involves regressive libidinal, pre-oedipal stages. In the torturer we do not know about his/her libidinal development but he/she is also often inflicting pain in erotogenic zones, which eventually, if not initially, may lead him/her to derive some sexual response and gratification.

The question is, was the torturer a perverse individual to begin with, or, did the corrupt, perverse circumstances superimpose a perverse condition on him? In psychodynamic terms we could speculate that a triangulation process was at work, in which the State (Father) was hiring him as an instrument of social perversion with a tremendous sense of ambiguity - enabling him to split off the image of Father as the tyrannical State and Mother as the denigrated and ravished Society on whose body he could, symbolically speaking, take revenge? Thus, instead of the immediate future punishment dreaded by the perverse individual, the torturer could look forward to rewards for 'good work'.

The Law

Just as the perverse individual is aware of the element of risk-taking, excitement and ambiguity, these mechanisms are also operating in the torturer's mind. Both are criminals insofar as torture is legally punishable; the Perverse State cannot be fully and permanently legalized although the torturer may delude himself as to the 'legality' of his actions. Procedures against universal law and human rights are enacted through secret directives only known by members of institutions in charge of their execution. The actual agents of the Perverse State, although feeling protected by the hierarchical structure going all the way up to the head of government, are simultaneously part of a conspiracy and knowingly act in defiance of the normal sentiments in society as enacted in law. This is a particularly difficult area to differentiate between the two groups.

The perverse individual 'knows' he is acting against society regardless of how much he tries to use very primitive defensive mechanisms such as denial, splitting, and projective identification. But the torturer believes he is acting as a 'legalized' agent for the State - which by now has been deeply intertwined in his mind with society. He is taking care of its welfare and survival through a perverse and perverting ideology, which operates through ambiguity but does not include ambivalence, often found in perverse behaviour. Both groups use encapsulation of these actions, enabling them to conceal their behaviours and actions from friends and family members. They try, and sometimes succeed, in showing themselves as "law abiding" citizens and "good and responsible" parents. The actions are uncovered in different ways: for the perverse individual by detection by society's agents; for the torturer by the change of the political-social regime.

Death and The Maiden

My exploration of these questions was very much enlightened by a play by a Chilean author, Ariel Dorfman, called "Death and the Maiden" which was performed by the Royal Court first upstairs and then very successfully in the downstairs main theatre. The play is about a man and wife. The wife had been raped, brutalized, and tortured 15 years ago under the Chilean military rule and still experiences a recurrent nightmare that her horrific experiences might be repeated despite the fact that she married a man who loves her very much, and on whom she relies completely for support. One day her husband returns from a political meeting - by now there is a democracy, an elected government - having been nominated to a government commission to investigate abuse of human rights. He had gotten a flat tyre on the motorway and was helped by a man who returned him safely home. During an animated scene on the doorstep, whilst the husband articulates his gratitude, and he and the stranger talk at great length, we see the wife being overtaken with bewilderment. We don't know what is going on until, a few hours later, the stranger (a doctor) appears at their house to congratulate the husband, having heard on the radio that he is now on a government commission.

Despite the time (it is 2am and the couple are in bed) the husband opens the door and invites the stranger to have a drink and then to sleep overnight in the house. The wife becomes extremely angry and very upset. She clubs the stranger and chains him to a chair and starts interrogating and torturing him. She has recognized this man as her torturer; a doctor who was at first sweet, nice, and compliant and yet committed the most terrible acts against her in the police station. The woman is now ready to take as much revenge as she can as all the pain has come rushing back. The husband is amazed at his wife's fury, and initially tries to convince her that she is mistaken about the identity of the friendly man but he eventually believes her.

Especially enlightening is a comment that the strange doctor makes towards the end of the play, after it has become apparent that he is indeed the torturer. In Act 3 he says:

The real truth, it was for humanitarian reasons. We're at war, I thought, they want to kill me and my family, they want to install a totalitarian dictatorship, but even so, they still have the right to some form of medical attention. It was slowly, almost without realizing how, that I became involved in more delicate operations, they let me sit in on sessions where my role was to determine if the prisoners could take that much torture, that much electric current. At first I told myself that it was a way of saving people's lives, and I did, because many times I told them - without it being true, simply to help the person who was being tortured - I ordered them to stop or the prisoner would die. But afterwards I began to - bit by bit, the virtue I was feeling turned into excitement - the mask of virtue fell off it and it, the excitement, it hid, it hid, it hid from me what I was doing, the swamp of what -. By the time Paulina Salas was brought in it was already too late. Too late - too late. A kind of - brutalization took over my life, I began to really truly like what I was doing. It became a game. My curiosity was partly morbid, partly scientific. How much can this woman take? More than the other one? Does her sex dry up when you put the current through her? Can she have an orgasm under those circumstances? She is entirely in your power, you can carry out all your fantasies, you can do what you want with her. Everything they have forbidden you since ever, whatever your mother ever urgently whispered you were never to do. [35]

It is quite obvious that the man had learned how to get secondary gain - sexual excitement and sexual gratification - from the acts of torture. This in itself had become a perversion, which is very much the outcome of obedience and compliance to the State.

In an interview Ariel Dorfman says that though he had had the subject in mind for a long time it was only in 1990 when Chile was allowed to have an elected government that he felt he had the appropriate background for the play. In his own words:

That kidnapping and trial would occur, not in a nation under the boot of a dictator, but in one that was in transition to democracy, where so many Chileans were grappling with the hidden traumas of what had been done to them while other Chileans wondered if their crimes would now be revealed. It also became clear that the way to make the husband of the tortured woman have a tremendous stake in the outcome of that kidnapping was to make him a member of a Commission similar to the one headed by Rettig..... I felt, however, that if as a citizen I had to be responsible and reasonable, as an artist I had to answer the wild mating call of my characters and break the silence which was weighing upon so many of my self-censored compatriots, fearful of creating 'trouble' for the new democracy. It was then and is now more than ever my belief that a fragile democracy is strengthened by expressing for all to see the deep dramas and sorrows and hopes that underlie its existence and that it is not by hiding the damage we have inflicted on ourselves that we will avoid its repetition.... How can those who tortured and those who were tortured co-exist in the same land? How to heal a country that has been traumatized by repression if the fear to speak out is still omnipresent everywhere? And how do you reach the truth if lying has become a habit? How do we keep the past alive without becoming its prisoner? How do we forget it without risking its repetition in the future? Is it legitimate to sacrifice the truth to ensure peace? And what are the consequences of suppressing that past and the truth it is whispering or howling to us? Are people free to search for justice and equality if the threat of a military intervention haunts them? And given these circumstances can violence be avoided? And how guilty are we all of what happened to those who suffered most? And perhaps the greatest dilemma of them all: how to confront these issues without destroying the national consensus which creates democratic stability?[36]

Notes

1. Deleuze, G., *Masochism*, New York: Zone Books, 1991, p. 67.

2. McDougall, J., *The Many Faces of Eros*, London: Free Association Books, 1995, p. 219.

3. Evans, P., 'Phantom Projection', *Tate Art Magazine*, Issue 26, Autumn 2001, p. 32.

4. Hopkins, D., 'Male Shots', *Tate Art Magazine*, Issue 26, Autumn 2001, pp. 24–8.

5. de Sade, A.D., *La Nouvelle Justine*, in Chasseguet- Smirgel, Janine, 'Reflexions on the Connexions Between Perversion and Sadism', *International Journal of Psycho- Analysis*, vol. 59, 1978, pp. 27–35 (p. 1).

6. Chasseguet-Smirgel, J., op. cit., pp. 31, 32 .

7. Carter, A., *The Sadeian Woman*, London: Virago, 1979, p. 27.

8. Andrews, N., 'Girls Just Want to End Oppression', *Financial Times*, FT Weekend, 13 April 2002, pp. 13–14. All subsequent information on *Baise-Moi* is drawn from this source.

9. Welldon, E.V., *Mother, Madonna, Whore: The Idealization and Denigration of Motherhood*, London: Free Association Books, 1988, p. 106.

10. Adapted from 'Sexual Masochism' entry, in

Diagnostic and Statistical Manual of Mental Disorders: DSM-IV, Fourth Edition, Washington DC: American Psychiatric Association, 1994, p. 529.

11. von Sacher-Masoch, L., in Deleuze, G., op. cit., p. 12.

12. Deleuze, G., op. cit., pp. 11, 12.

13. Ibid., p. 71.

14. Ibid., p. 12.

15. Reik, T., *Masochism in Modern Man* (1957), in Isaacs, A. (ed.), *The Cassell Dictionary of Sex Quotations*, London: Cassell, 1997, pp. 228–9.

16. Stoller, R.J., *Perversion* (1976), in Isaacs, A., op. cit., pp. 229–9.

17. Loewenstein, R.M., *A Contribution to the Psycho- analytic Theory of Masochism*, (1956), in Isaacs, A., op. cit., pp. 228–9.

18. Deleuze, G., op. cit., p. 20.

19. Strenger, C., *Individuality: The Impossible Project*, Madison, CT: International Universities Press, Inc., 1998, p. 135–44 (p. 138).

20. West, F., in Masters, B., *'She Must Have Known': The Trial of Rosemary West*, London: Doubleday, 1996, p. 127.

21. Fromm, E., *The Heart of Man* (1964), in Isaacs, A., op. cit., pp. 228–9.

22. Welldon, E.V., 'Contrasts in Male and Female

Perversions', in Cordess, C., and Cox, M. (eds.), *Forensic Psychotherapy*, London: Jessica Kingsley Publishers, 1996, pp. 273–89 .

23. Bernardez, T., 'Women and Anger: Conflicts with Aggression in Contemporary Women', *Journal of the American Medical Association*, vol. 33, 1987, pp. 215–19.

24. Welldon, E.V., 'Women as Abusers', in *Planning Mental Health Services for Women: A Multi-Professional Handbook*, London: Routledge, 1996, pp. 176–89.

25. McDougall, J., *Theatres of the Body: A Psychoanalytic Approach to Psychosomatic Illness*, New York/London: Norton, 1989, p. 28.

26. Welldon, E.V., 'Bodies Across Generations and Cycles of Abuse', in Molfino, F., and Zanardi, C. (eds.), *Symptoms, Body, Femininity: From Hysteria to Bulimia*, Bologna: CLUEB, 1999, pp. 327–46 (p. 333).

27. Welldon, E.V., 'Female Perversion and Hysteria', *British Journal of Psychotherapy*, vol. XI, no. 3, 1995, pp. 406–14 (p. 408).

28. Hermann, I., 'Clinging-Going-in-Search', *Psychoanalytic Quarterly*, vol. 45, 1976, pp. 5–36.

29. Glasser, M., 'Some aspects of the role of aggression in the perversions', in I. Rosen (ed.),

Sexual Deviations. Oxford: OUP.

30. Welldon, E.V. (1988), op. cit., p. 72.

31. West, F., in Masters, B., op. cit., p. 115.

32. Welldon, E.V., 'Let the Treatment Fit the Crime', 20th Foulkes Lecture; also published in *Group Analysis*, vol. 30, 1997, pp. 9–26.

33. Puget, J., *Social violence and psychoanalysis in Argentina*, Free Associations 13, 1988.

34. Welldon, E.V. (1988), op. cit.

35. Dorfman, A, *Death and the Maiden: a Play in Three Acts*, Nick Hern Books, London, 1991.

36. Ibid., afterword

Further Reading

Andrews, N., 'Girls Just Want to End Oppression', *Financial Times*, FT weekend, 13 April 2002, pp. 13–14.

Bernardez, T., 'Women and Anger: Conflicts with Aggression in Contemporary Women', *Journal of the American Medical Association*, vol. 33, 1987, pp. 215–19.

Carter, A., *The Sadeian Woman*, London: Virago, 1979. Chasseguet-Smirgel, J., 'Reflexions on the Connexions Between Perversion and Sadism', *International*

Journal of Psycho-Analysis, vol. 59, 1978, pp. 27–35. Deleuze, G., *Masochism*, New York: Zone Books, 1991. *Diagnostic and Statistical Manual of Mental Disorders*,

Fourth Edition, Washington DC: American Psychi-atric Association, 1994. Evans, P., 'Phantom Projection', *Tate Art Magazine*,

Issue 26, Autumn 2001, p. 32. Fogel, G., and Myers, W.A. (eds.), *Perversions and Near*

Perversions In Clinical Practice, New Psychoanalytical

Perspectives, New Haven, CT: Yale University, 1991. Fromm, E., *The Heart of Man* (1964), London:

HarperCollins, 1980. Garland, C. (ed.), *Understanding Trauma: A Psycho-analytic Approach*, London: Duckworth, 1998.

Gilligan, J., *Violence: Our Deadly Epidemic and Its Causes*, New York: Putnam, 1996.

Hermann, I., 'Clinging-Going-in-Search', *Psychoanalytic Quarterly*, vol. 45, 1976, pp. 5–36.

Hopkins, D., 'Male Shots', *Tate Art Magazine*, Issue 26, Autumn 2001, pp. 24–8.

Hopper, E., 'On the Nature of Hope in Psychoanalysis', *British Journal of Psychotherapy*, vol. XVIII, no. 2, 2001, pp. 205–226.

von Krafft-Ebing, R., *Psychopathia Sexualis* (1886), London: Creation Books, 1997.

Masters, B., *'She Must Have Known': The Trial of Rosemary West*, London: Doubleday, 1996.

Matthews, R., Matthews, J.K., and Speltz, K., *Female Sexual Offenders: An Exploratory Study*, Orwell, VT: Safer Society Press, 1989.

McDougall, J., *Theatres of the Body: A Psychoanalytic Approach to Psychosomatic Illness*, New York/ London: Norton, 1989.

—— *The Many Faces of Eros*, London: Free Association Books, 1995.

Montgomery, J.D., and Greif, A.C., *Masochism: The Treatment of Self-inflicted Suffering*, Madison,

CT: International Universities Press, 1989.

Novick, J., and Novick, K.K., *Fearful Symmetry: The Development and Treatment of Sadomasochism*, Northvale, NJ: Jason Aronson, 1996.

von Sacher-Masoch, L., *Venus in Furs* (1870), Harmondsworth: Penguin, 2000.

de Sade, M., *Justine, Philosophy in the Bedroom and Other Writings*, New York: Grove Press/Atlantic Monthly Press, 2000.

—— *The 120 Days of Sodom* (1785), London: Arrow Books, 1991.

—— *Juliette* (1798), trans. A. Wainhouse, London: Arrow Books, 1991.

Stoller, R., *Observing the Erotic Imagination*, New Haven, CT: Yale University Press, 1985.

Strenger, C., *Individuality: The Impossible Project*, Madison, CT: International Universities Press, Inc., 1998, p. 135–44.

Verhaeghe, P., *Beyond Gender: From Subject to Drive*, New York: Other Press, 2001.

Welldon, E.V., *Mother, Madonna, Whore: The Idealiz- ation and Denigration of Motherhood*, London: Free Association Books, 1988; current American Edition, Guilford Press, 1992.

—— 'Contrasts in Male and Female Perversions', in Cordess, C., and Cox, M. (eds.), *Forensic Psycho-*

therapy, London: Jessica Kingsley Publishers, 1996, pp. 273–89.

—— 'Women as Abusers', in Abel, K., et al., *Planning Mental Health Services for Women: A Multi- Professional Handbook*, London: Routledge, 1996, pp. 176–89.

—— 'Let the Treatment Fit the Crime', 20th Foulkes Lecture, also published in *Group Analysis*, vol. 30, 1997, pp. 9–26.

—— 'Bodies Across Generations and Cycles of Abuse', in Molfino, F., and Zanardi, C. (eds.), *Symptoms, Body, Femininity: From Hysteria to Bulimia*, Bologna: CLUEB, 1999, pp. 327–46.

—— 'Babies as Transitional Objects', in Brett Kahr (ed.), *Forensic Psychotherapy and Psychopathology: Winnicottian Perspectives*, London: Karnac Books, 2001.

Welldon, E.V. and Van Velsen, C. (eds.), *A Practical Guide to Forensic Psychotherapy*, London: Jessica Kingsley Publishers, 1997.

De Zulueta, F., *From Pain to Violence: The Traumatic Roots of Destructiveness*, London: Whurr, 1993.

ABOUT THE AUTHOR

Dr Estela V. Welldon, MD, HonDSc, FRCPsych, Hon.Memb. APsaA, is an Honorary Consultant Psychiatrist in Psychotherapy at Tavistock and Portman NHS Clinics. She is the founder and Honorary Life President of the International Association for Forensic Psychotherapy, and has an Honorary Doctorate in Science from Oxford Brookes University. She is a Member of the British Association for Psychotherapy, the British Psychoanalytic Council, the Institute of Group Analysis, the American Group Psychotherapy Association, and the International Association for Group Psychotherapy, and is an Honorary member of the Society of Couple Psychoanalytic Psychotherapists, Tavistock Clinic. She works privately as a psychoanalytic psychotherapist and lectures worldwide. She is the author of *Mother, Madonna, Whore: The Idealization and Denigration of Motherhood* (1988), *Ideas in Psychoanalysis: Sadomasochism* (2002), *Playing with Dynamite: A Personal Approach to the Psychoanalytic Understanding of Perversions, Violence, and Criminality* (2011), and is the main editor of *A Practical Guide to Forensic Psychotherapy* (1997).